Congratulatyions

poems by
Tyler James Davis

Puttertutters Press

Mahanoy City : Bethlehem : Woodbridge : a hot shower

If you purchased this book without a cover, you have gone too far in your search for bargain-priced books. The extra dollar or two per book is worth it if the covers are intact.

WARNING: This poetry book contains adult content not suitable for children. Puttertutters Press is travelling coast to coast meeting the cutest, sexiest poems in the country to find the hottest poem in America. These are the kinds of poems you've always wanted to meet, just the way you like them – free verse and ready to go wild! Puttertutters Press' *Congratulatyions*, now on VHS and DVD for only $12!

You could probably handle the truth, to be quite honest.

The design of this cover was actually an original creation, if you can believe that. Tyler is glad that his previous two books weren't mainstream popular because he could have gotten into trouble for copyright infringement. Even though Tyler had streamed WWE PPVs for 3 years and torrented gigs upon gigs of movies, songs, and programs in his younger days, the only time he got into trouble was when he torrented *American Gangster* and his internet provider emailed him and told him to delete the file. He didn't even watch the movie, either, so it was a waste of a strike on his internet account.

Cover Design by Tyler James Davis
Published by Puttertutters Press.
"This is the best I got!"

15 14 13 12 11 10 9 8 7 6 5 4 3 2 1 happy new year!

ISBN: 0692101381
ISBN-13: 978-0692101384

THANKS TO

you.

HOLY CRAP, IT'S BOOK #3

Really, not much has changed since the last book. I still really miss a lot of things from my childhood, and I wrote poems about those things. I still think nature is neat, and I wrote some poems about how I feel about nature. I still greatly enjoy the existence of cats, and I wrote some poems about the magnificence of cats. I still can't get over the girl I liked in high school, and I wrote some poems about how I feel. There are some other existential things in there, too, just like last time. I stayed very much on-brand with this book.

For part of this book, I took a bunch of old tweets and used them as poemseeds. It was hard to go from 27,000 tweets to the ~40 poems that ended up being derived from tweets, especially because all of my tweets are hilarious and profound and I wanted everyone to see all of them, which is hard to do when my account is private.

I don't think I have anything left to write poems about after this. I covered it all. I've done all there is to do. I will experience nothing new in my life that will warrant unique feelings and thoughts that will cause me to rethink my personal philosophy and approach to life, get all emotional and sappy, and feel the urge to write about it all.

That's pretty much all I had to say.

Nothing new over here.

So, what's new with you?

CONGRATULATYIONS

CONGRATULATYIONS

Trinkets, Talismans, and Tchotchkes

I'm a big fan of having something
to show for all your work,
some sort of gift shop tchotchke
consolation prize from any given memory
that is a portkey to everything
that was unfurled then and there,
whether it's a t-shirt from the bar
you visited during senior week,
or a shot glass from the zoo
you were a chaperone on
for your class' field trip,
or just a photograph you took
from your exclusive vantage point,
or you can have some kind of parting gift,
like a quantitative piece of datum
that says exactly how you were or how it was
that you can objectively put up
against someone else's results
for an undeniable comparison
to say that yours was better
and there's an incontrovertible "best."

I'm finding that a lot of my experiences with people
have been worked on and used in the moment,
but are then tossed away like a sketch of a whale
that you just keep messing up on
and have no reason to keep,
because you have a whole pad of paper
to start a newer version
where the proportions are much better
and there isn't so much erasing,
and you can't see all the quick light lines
that helped make the thicker pen lines
that would mark the final version.

You were too busy waiting for
the "perfect" of your target
that it started to go further away,
and you realized that the perfect had passed
and you should have done something with
the "pretty good" of your target,
but you were too greedy
because you were too willing
to see the imperfect in something perfect,
and how misguided that was,
that you misplaced too much confidence in them
to be all the best that they could be.

So now you're just taking what you can get,
which is an imitation of what you wanted
and pictured in your mind
when you were waiting for the ideal form to exist,
and now some of the details might be muddied,
looking at the past as an impressionist painting,

So you're reeling in your line
at the first bite of the bait
because you'll settle now
for anything above a boot and a tire
as long as it's a fish,
even if it's not the record-breaker
you knew you were close to nabbing
a few years ago,
because it got away,
or rather,
before it even
came close
to your hook
to bite.

Hi-8

I'm archiving old Hi-8 video tapes
from when I was 13
and thought that
recording my friends
playing with scooters
and pogo sticks
in the street at night
with night vision on
and the LCD screen turned around
so they can see themselves
made me the über-coolest,

and I'm studying the unique situations
like I'm a football player
studying tape in the locker room,
reviewing plays from a game
so they can be more efficiently run
next week in a game
that will have the same winning parameters,
whereas I don't even know if there will be a next game,
or what sport it might be,
or if there will be any fans sticking around
to cheer me on this time
should I succeed in any aspects of my life,

and I catch myself responding
(in my head)
to moments in the video
with the same quips
past-me on the tape responds with
1 second later,

and I don't know if I should be happy
that my response then
was the best response

I could think of now,
or sad that my response now
was no better than my response then.

There Is No Season Finale

Let me find some walls
that I can put around me.
Let me find a door
to connect me to outside.
Let me walk the hall
to the places I want to be.
Let me find someone
to be there at my side.

Let me have a clock
to see the time go by.
Let me find a corner
that will be where I can hide.
Let me find a book
that will answer my question "why?"
Let me find the strength
to then go outside.

This will all be said
with the same detached halfmumble
as the Nicene Creed is said at Mass,
where your vocal cords are barely vibrating
to get the gravelly vowels out,
and not much attention is being paid
to what you're praying for
because you've said it 52+ times a year
for the past howevermany years you've been alive,
and you're sort of holding out
that you'll be granted the courage and serenity
and everything else in your toolbelt of faith
to give you a piece of an epiphany.

We had been lied to
that there is a gift shop of treasures
at the end of the museum tour,

so we're stealing bones from a T. Rex
and pelts from a pioneer mannequin
and we're revving our engines
and turning the shower water temperature to scalding
before we pass through the curtain
to the tepid bathroom air
that gets colder in comparison
as the water gets hotter,
because we're searching for a quick kick
which won't seem so significant
when there's another needed extra kick
coming right after,
and the cliff we're facing
gets bigger as we climb
to try to get a better view
of what we thought we might see
just before we break through the clouds.

Memorial Day

A single police car
would move up the street,
the officer's feet off the pedals,
letting you know
that what you were about to see
was the officially-sanctioned-by-the-borough
Memorial Day parade.

The Mahanoy Area HS marching band was next,
playing the same song as last time,
and we would fawn over the hot public school girls
who weren't banned by their moms
from using makeup.

The T-ball players drowned
in their youth large uniform t-shirts.
They were sitting in the bed of a pickup truck,
tossing out candy,
scattering it like buckshot
in the general direction
of the children standing
at the street corners,
inevitably hitting my mom's car
with a hail of
Dubble Bubble and
Tootsie Rolls
in the process.

I got to be part of the pageant and spectacle
during my 3 years as a Little Leaguer,
marching in the back-right corner of our company,
my cleats clopping on the macadam
as I curled the brim of my hat
by putting it in a vise
between my two palms.

Our coaches were mainstays in the local community,
and we treated every wave at them
as a wave at us,
winding up our ego a click at a time.

We wouldn't see any of our friends along the route,
because they were also on a Little League team,
marching somewhere else in the parade,
so we were there to be seen by the adults
as a reassurance that our town had a future
that hopefully wouldn't move out after high school.

The firetrucks were behind us,
honking their phlegm-throated horns
and whooping their special sirens
over their already-wailing regular sirens
as they trotted along,
their diesel fumes smogging up the air
like the incense at Benediction.

The townspeople on porches
and those slouching in lawn chairs at the curb
would thank the firefighters with waves
for protecting the town
from the blighted firetrap rowhomes
that would catch fire with enough frequency
to instill in you the fear
that any object in your house
could burst into flames at any moment,
no matter how illogical it might seem,
and burn down the whole block,
because fire was the Devil
in our town of rowhomes,
and even though I check
my smoke detector batteries
twice every year
(when you change your clocks for daylight savings time),

I know that a perfect storm of failures
can and will occur
and cause a spark
that starts a fire
that will burn down half the town
despite the best efforts of our volunteer fire departments
and those of the towns around us,

because they can't stop every fire from happening,

no matter how successful their bazaars are

or how many contests they've held at the schools
where you draw a map of your family's fire escape plan

or how much money they collected
for the town fireworks
that have been slowly glowing up the sky
less and less in recent years

or how many fireman's convention trophies they've won

or how nicely they march in the
Memorial Day parade.

All of our marching in parades backfired,
because we got a chance to see
how sort-of-but-not-really rundown the town was
when we were only kids
and could compare its state then
to what we saw 8 years later
as the college acceptance letters rolled in
and the husks of homes stood
as windowless remnants
like the skin on cooked-for-too-long
baked potato wedges.

Children of Carbon

The youth
and the hope for tomorrow
fled the area,

sick of waiting through
the heat and pressure.

The biggest lie we believed
was that coal becomes diamonds
in time.

St. Bartholomew

The Eastern European immigrants
didn't think of the logistics
of how you can un-make a church
when they were erecting
St. Bartholomew's in Brockton.

The excess rock
from the coal mine in the mountain
was carried by donkeys and carts
down the slope
to form the new church's foundation
next to the freshly burned down husk
of the last St. Bartholomew's
so they could be ready
in time for the annual Christmas program.

Brockton built their church
on the rock of their faith
that the anthracite coal will be wanted
for as long as it could burn,
and that their children's children
would be as coalblind as they were
that they'd stick around
and hope for the best
while their prayers were sent up
into the atmosphere
as they were walled in
by burnt coaldust culm piles
growing by the minute
in all the patch towns
around them.

Risk

I'm searching eBay
for the 1975 version of Risk,
because I'm trying to re-collect
the stash of board games
I used to have
on the shelf in my bedroom closet
before my parents decided
to throw them all away
by leaving them unbagged on the curb
before I left for school one morning.

The collection of games
was my way to lure friends over my house,
or to get invited somewhere else
with a game or two in tow,
and when those games were gone
I had to find something else physical
to attach to my being
that I could accompany elsewhere
as its +1.

I had my camcorder in late elementary school
and then a Wii in high school,

and then there was a point where the interest
in all of those items waned,
and I built my own self up
as the reason for having me somewhere,
which ended up being enough of a reason
for me to be invited to *Guitar Hero II* parties
and other parties
where a friend got a case of beer
and 2 handles of UV Blue and Captain
and our group of friends
drank in her living room

and slept under afghan blankets
with musty pillows propped up
against the china cabinets
filled with antique cheese dishes.

I want to be somewhere
based on my own merits
and not because of an asterisk-included
contractual obligation.

Now that friends are farther & further away,
getting together with others
takes more than personalities
and wanting to sew together
the gap of time between seeing each other,
so there needs to be some gimmicks again
to overcome the larger hurdles
between stasis and travel.

I can't wait until this copy of Risk comes in next week
and be the topic of cancelled plans
that were never going to happen anyway
regardless of the board games under my bed.

Exhibit A

Maybe if I buy enough things
to put on display in my room
then any girls that end up there
who take a look around
will have to spend enough time
that we enter a common-law marriage
before she realizes she has only seen
one wall of my room
(which is covered with old newspaper clippings
of noteworthy moments
in dirigible aviation history)
and that we haven't even touched
on the very lengthy back stories
that each and every book
on my IKEA bookshelf
(that I put together on my own)
has.

Now That I'm Here

i'm afraid that i want to live here my whole life
and my body is doing the suddenjump
when you slip into sleep too quickly
and you brace for the fall into infinity
despite being the safest you can be,
and i'm catching myself wanting to catch myself
dwelling in frustration of made up situations
that i can summon when i need them
to have something to fall back on
when i'm getting too antsy from being too happy.

i'm always suspicious when things are overly-okay,
like when you're on the same road for a while
when you're going somewhere unknown,
and you have to check your GPS in a huff,
expecting to see a turn in 250 feet
that you hadn't been warned about,
or when the sun is slightly rising
on a weekday and you're still in bed
and you panic-check your phone
to see if you overslept
due to your a.m. alarms being set as p.m.

there's everything abiotic that i need here.
my friends are all 4 hours up 95,
and i never see them when i'm back in PA,
so why does it matter how far i live from them anyway?
i often make plans to see those i knew from high school,
but those always fall through,
because the details were always so structurally unsound.

Looking Glass Glasses

I peek too often
at my opponents' screens
during split screen multiplayer
and I forget which one is mine,
so I'm running into a wall
while getting grenades thrown at me
because I think I'm the guy
in the upper right screen
that's getting double kills nonstop.

I pay more attention
to what place I'm in
in racing games
than I do actually racing
and trying to maintain/improve my standings,
because even if I don't win,
at least I have those moments where I'm doing well
and I put them in amber to keep forever
as some consolation prize
when I inevitably lose
because I don't practice any skills necessary to do well,
but try to get by on the mistakes of others.

My Time

I can't wait
until I'm the one
that the fates decide
is going to get a reward
for all of these things
I work toward
and care about,

and you're doing to say,
"wow,
Tyler is so
annoying,
he's so positive
all of the time,
like,
'calm down already,'
right?"

and I'm going to rub it in all of your faces
and parade it around
like how the Italians parade around
the statue of Mary,

and I'm going to place ads
targeting you all on Facebook,

and I'll put full-page ads
in the *Republican Herald*
and *Times News*,

and I'll go on *Late Night with Stephen Colbert*
in the 2nd guest segment spot
and talk about it all
for my allotted 8 minutes
to tell everyone else.

Flukes

Holding out
for a series of flukes
in my favor.

Recursive Nostalgia

If you spend today remembering yesterday,
what will you remember tomorrow?

Denouement

There's
always
a
day
after
the
happiest
day
of
your
life.

Nothing You Do Is Unimportant

You know the feeling that compels you
to buy lemonade from a kid's lemonade stand?

It's seeing someone care so much
and wanting to show support.

It's not pity,
because you don't feel sad –
you feel happy that someone is outwardly being them
and you want to support that honesty.

Something seems cheap or crappy or not quite right,
but it's a genuine and authentic and pure
form of their passion.

I feel so weird when people care about something.
I always feel like it isn't genuine.

I'm so love shy.

I'm so pessimistic and dismissive.

I hate when something comes across as pitiful,
because I can empathize with that so much
with things I've made and parties I've had.

One time when I was 11,
my dad was late picking me up
for a Little League game,
but it was because he was picking me up
a Gatorade in my favorite flavor,
and I got upset at him for being late
and I didn't appreciate the thought that he was putting
into getting the Gatorade.

Think of how much care and work and time
goes into every detail of everything you use.
You're worth all of those people's sweat and energy.

I hate when there's a discrepancy
between how much two people care
about the same thing.

Refraction of Dedication

I hate seeing something
that's a relic
of when some people
cared a whole lot
about 1 thing
and they cared enough
to bring that object
into existence
as a symbol of
how hopeful
and naïve
they were

that they'd always care
and their kids would care
and more people would come along
who also care
as much as they cared
when they focused
all of their energy and time
through a magnifying glass
to refract their dedication
into 1 single spot of hyperbright light.

Eventual Stairway

I'm listening to a Led Zeppelin bootleg
where they're trying to figure out
how to play "Stairway to Heaven"
because they're living in a world
that didn't have "Stairway to Heaven,"
so they had to step up and create it.

The logistics and minutiae
were still being worked out,
and they probably didn't know
how much importance the song will have
and how much it will displace other songs
(like the milk in a glass when you dip in a cookie)
because this song is a fresh and soft cookie
with chocolate chips the size of a Hershey's Kiss.

They're playing the song wrong
because they don't know what the song yet is,
but each time they start over and play new take,
you can see a glimmer of a trait
that is more similar to the final version,
and you want to call out in affirmation
that they're on the right path,
like you're watching a friend struggle
via a crystal ball in an evil wizard's lair
and you don't want them to give up
going through the labyrinth that leads to the castle.

Unlike real life,
I can look at the band's struggle
and not worry
because I know they achieve their end goal.

It makes me think about everything that I do,
because I don't know which beginnings

will arrive at their destinations,
and I don't know what degree of completeness
some actions will have,
and I don't know if there was more perfection
a little further down the path,
and I don't know what will eventually happen
until it happens,
and I don't know how it'll be received
until it is presented,
and I don't know to what amount
it will be remarkable,
but every opportunity is a fresh chance
and it makes me wonder:

Have I been close to my "Stairway" but given up?
and
What will my eventual "Stairway" be?

Credits

We all do something notable
in the lives of everyone
that we come in contact with,

and I'm only hoping
that I get an
executive producer credit
on a couple people's movies,

or maybe a
director of photography credit
that still puts me 2 or 3 names
from the top
of the scroll at the end,

because I'm trying to avoid
being one of those names
that pops up
5 minutes deep
as the 2nd unit
lighting grip,

by which point
the names are
stacked 3 wide
and are only seen by
the movie theater ushers
(who are sweeping up the popcorn
and dropping one-fourth-full cups of soda
into their garbage bags)
and by the superfans waiting
to see if there's a post-credits scene
(but there isn't).

Completionist

Some people can count
from 1 to 2
and not even think
about the fact
that there are
an
infinite
number of numbers
between them,

and I catch myself
trying to go through them all
like I'm a completionist
playing a video game
collecting all 12,000 gems
or all 100 hidden packages
and considering myself a failure
if I don't get them all,
throwing the game's purpose
out the window
so I can turn fun and success
into some quantitative measurement.

I believe that there is a
perfect arrangement of your belongings
when you have to pack a bag
before going on a trip,
and I will help the items
realize their perfect potential
so that I can wholly complete
some missions in my life
on my quest to 100%.

However, when I see others doing this,
I am a hypocrite

that thinks they are breeding anxiety
by living every outcome
of their hypothetical bracket of choices
and talking about options
and variables
and pathways
that may not even exist,
which only wastes energy
that won't be
rewarded or recouped later.

Re

I wish I could
do some things
for the first time again.

I wish I could
do some things
for the last time for once.

Caught 'em All

I finished my
Pokémon trading card sets
today

after having some
open windows
that stayed vacant
for too long
in my card binder pages

in the sections
of the later sets
that I collected
while also discovering
how pretty girls' smiles could be.

I got
Brock's Ninetales,
Koga's Ditto,
and a Misty trainer card
from different people on eBay
for maybe $20 in total

and I was able to close
one of the many open doors
from when I was younger
and finish
one of the
actually-finishable
still-pending missions
whose time limit
hadn't yet expired.

On/Off

I'm walking into my bedroom
and I reach to the left
to flick on the light switch,
but I miss,
so I try to swipe it down again
(while still continuing to walk into the room)
and I miss again
(because I kept going)
and didn't take the time to pause,
so I spread open my hand
and paw at the switch,
but I'm too far away to reach it
(because I'm several steps into the room)
and I'm a recalculating GPS
because I've invested too much time now
(walking into the room)
to go back and turn on the lights
that I'm telling myself
(in a very sour grapes kind-of-way)
I don't need light at all
because I actually can see in low light
the way cats can see shadows,
so I'll just bump into my dresser a couple times
with the acromion of my shoulder as the battering ram
and misplace my jacket
on where I thought my desk chair was,
because that's the consequence of the actions I make
without thinking of the consequences,
and it's 14 years later
and I still haven't stubbed my toe on my bed
to get an initial clue of where it might be,
so I haven't slept at all,
and the light switch
is still in the opposite direction of where I want to be,
which is probably a good thing

because my eyes finally did slightly adjust
to the lack of light,
and flipping the switch on
will only disorient me
all over again.

Being Alone Makes Me Feel Less Alone

On the cover of the *Animorphs* book,
where the girl is turning into a llama,
I'm at about the 3rd of 5 phases
where I'm the girl
and the llama represents the feeling
of an oxymoronic public isolation
that homeless people must feel.

"There has to be a reason
that no one else wants
to eat at Panera with him,
even when he's using a gift card
with over $25 still left on it"
they all ponder
as I sit at 1 of the 3
2-person tables in the restaurant.

It's a faux pas for me
to even look at anyone,
because that nonconsensually involves them
in my silent wallowing of solitude
and they feel a magnetic pull towards me
like when you get a belt loop stuck
on the handle of a kitchen cabinet
and panic with a yelp
when you're tugged back.

I have nothing
that I'm allowed to look at,
except the table
and the floor
and the wall
within a 2 foot radius around me,
like I'm hiding under a cardboard box
that your fridge came in,

but never to pop out in surprise,
lest I make it seem to those around me
that I'm listening in
or trying to join their exclusive conversation.

I'm too proud
to get a take-out meal
somewhere where they don't customarily ask
if you're dining in or taking out,
because that's admitting defeat and walking out
like a foreigner who doesn't know where my place is
(scarfing down a sandwich
in the warm 2700K lamp lights
at the undecorated table
in my house).

I'll rise above the expectations
of where a solo late-20s male
can publicly eat
by eating alone at Chipotle
(but still somewhere at
a table out of the way
where people can't too easily see me).

Hiding

We all need to sometimes hide,

like storage boxes do in the basement,

TV cables under a carpet,

the worries of something new
behind doing something familiar,

the drool-covered pillowcase
at the bottom of my hamper
under dirty socks and shorts
from the last time it was above 75 degrees,

and the salsa at the back of the fridge
from that party we had
3 months ago.

Still

I'm at the Post Office
trying to mail
a bootleg vinyl copy of
The Life of Pablo
that I bought on eBay
and now had to resell
because there were scratches on both discs
that prevented them from playing all the way through

and I'm waiting a
socially-acceptable distance
behind the lady at the counter
who is mailing a package to Germany.

The cashier says "ah, Deutschland?"
and she says "huh?"
and he says he always vacations there
and they start conversing in German
because he takes skiing vacations
in the same area
where her parents still live,

and I have to play the role
of someone who knows what's happening
but stays in a stasis
like the next character
on a video game's character select screen,
posed in partial shadow
because my presence isn't needed,
and I have to reduce all of my reasons of being
to mere existence.

I'm later caught in another limbo
when I go to give the cashier my money
but he's not yet ready for it

because he's waiting for the shipping label to print
and I'm forced to rest
the edge of my wrist on the counter
and fake a sniffle
to fill the silence
as part of my idle animation.

Proprietorship

I don't think
I can ever see myself
being responsible for
anyone or anything else but myself.

I'm doing everything for me
and for my own sake
and to reach my own
self-imposed ends.

No one owns
any stock in me.

I
just
sorta
wanna
do my own thing
forever.

Lost Boys

I don't think I'll ever grow up
or ever stop liking things I've liked before.

Saccharine

Everyone
has their own specific flavor of nostalgia,
a combination of 256 different elements,
mixed together like candy in a bag
that you pay per ounce for
at a semi-upscale outdoor mall's
confectionary emporium
where the shelves of candy
are all below eye level
because they aren't designed
with your gaze in mind anymore.

Mother Teresa of Calcutta

I was almost 5 years old
when "Living Saint" Mother Teresa
visited Mahanoy City
to see her Missionaries of Charity nuns
and I got to play a pick-up game
of wiffleball in the blocked-off street
in front of my house.

Her sisters
would walk around town
in their white saris
with three blue stripes at the edges
and I would wish them good mornings
and let them know I went to the Catholic school,
and that no, I did not have a rosary,
and yes, I would like to have one they made.

There were no parked cars because of her visit,
which meant no Pabst Blue Ribbon truck
parked in front of Blind Mike's house
and no seemingly-perpetually parked
Buick LeSabres
belonging to old ladies
who always got mad
when a wiffle ball
or Frisbee
or Nerf Vortex football
hit their hubcaps.

During the wiffleball game
I learned
that you don't have to run
to the pitcher's mound
between 1st and 2nd base,
which was one less thing

that I could do
later in life
to embarrass myself
in front of others who were
cooler and more with-it
than I was.

Thanks, Mother Teresa,
for the beads and the baseball,
and another event in my town's past
that we cling onto for relevancy.

What I Learned from the Boy Scouts

One of the guys
from the Boy Scouts
would come to our school
every single year
and talk to the boys in our class
out in the hallway
about how we should join the Tiger Scouts,
or whatever the 9-year-old equivalent was,

and every single year
they would tell us
that you only have to be
14 years old
to fly solo on an airplane,
and I had no idea what that meant,
because I kept picturing myself
playing violin alone in the aisle
and wondering why
no one under 14 years old
was allowed to do so,

and every single year
they would give us the
sign-up form
and would have us fold it
into a square the size of a Chiclet
and put it into our sock
so we couldn't possibly lose it
between now and getting home.

I used this same
"keep something safe in your sock" method
a couple years later
when we went on a field trip
to some museum

and our blue ABVM gym uniform sweatpants
had no pockets,
so I had to keep my souvenir money
somewhere different,
so I put about $5 in change in my sock
and had to get my right foot
completely butt-naked
in the hallway
next to the penny-squishing machine
when I wanted to buy one of those
purple velvet baggies
of cool shiny rocks.

Shrine of Perpetual Adoration

Sometime during the school year
in between all of the visits
for Stations of the Cross,

we marched down to St. Joseph's
to kneel and pray in silence
at the Shrine of Perpetual Adoration

where a consecrated host,
which is 100% Jesus' flesh
right there in front of us
looking like a circle wafer
(which is what it is
if you don't have any faith),

is embraced in the monstrance,
which is a starburst of metal
with rays of gold shooting out

like you looked directly at the Sun
when you tried to see
if the red light in front of you
turned green yet,
but moved your head too much
and the Sun peeked out
from behind the traffic light
and sizzled away at your rods and cones.

We went down the stairs
into the annex to the rectory
and we were washed over by
that ten-degree-cooler feeling
you get when you go somewhere subterranean.

Mrs. Purcell or Mrs. Habel
or whoever our teacher was that year
told us to scoot down the pews
until they were all full,
and I ended up in the 4th row from the back,
which was the 3rd row from the front,
because this room was smaller
than a zoo's gift shop.

While we pretended to
say the rosary silently to ourselves
(because Jesus apparently has strict rules
about not talking in his presence),
our fingers strafed across the rosary beads
at a pace that seemed
to be at the Goldilocks' Zone
while our eyes darted around the room
to avoid making eye contact
with the host
in the monstrance
on the altar
at the front of the room.

I'm 11 years old
and Jesus is there in front of me,
and I have nothing urgent to say.

Limited Edition

I like when characters
in movies and TV shows
wear some out-of-the-ordinary outfit
for a scene or an episode,
which gets memorialized months later
when a Comic-Con Exclusive action figure
of their character wearing that outfit
is debuted,
causing fans to flock
for the limited-edition merch,
which is a permanent secret handshake
that shows they're a more advanced fan
than those who forgot
something that happened differently
for 0.1% of the regular duration.

I'm glad that limited editions
aren't captured forever
in our own lives,
because I don't want
a PopVinyl figure out there
of me at my Confirmation,
where I got a haircut the same day
from the 90-year-old barber
who cut it so it only looked normal
with a part in the middle of my hair
which caused me to
cry for an hour
and show up to the church
with my eyes still red
and a nose filled with enough fuel
to have me sniffling all night.

Knoebels

You slip into sleep
just as easily
as you enter
Knoebels Amusement Resort
and feel in danger
of being crushed
by the swinging Galleon ship
when it inevitably falls off the support
as you're directly under the keel.

I'm in 6th grade
and an optional trip to Knoebels
is how we traditionally end the school year
after the 11 a.m. dismissal
on the real last day
the day before.

There's a new ride near the Merry Mixer
that's like one you'd find at Dorney,
which is why we skipped it.

My dad is swaddled in the carousel organ
and the sounds that will surely greet him
at the gates of heaven.

I want to play mini-golf,
but we didn't buy an all-day handstamp
for me to play mini-golf
(so says my whole family),
so I'm not going to get to play mini-golf.

I think a black widow bit me
halfway up the climb
to the top of the Sky Slide
on the metal spiral staircase.

The 8th grade girl that I had a crush on
wanted to know if I wanted to go
on the Sklooosh with her,
and I acted like the biggest fan of the Sklooosh
even though I've always been afraid to ride the Sklooosh,
and then I went on the Sklooosh with her
and we got drenched with the same wave of water
while I acted like I wasn't about to
barf up the 3 hot dogs I ate
earlier in the day
at the pavilion that our school reserved
for the end-of-the-year picnic.

The outdoor puppet theater
was doing *The Hobbit*
and all I could look at
was the hand of the puppeteer
and the marionette's control bar
dipping past the proscenium arch
down from the flyspace
whenever the Bilbo purposefully fell down
during one of his dance numbers.

A few trips ago,
I started to be over the maximum heights
for a lot of the rides I used to like,
and I'm realizing now
that I didn't ease myself
into being introduced properly
to the other rides I should be on,
like the Salt & Pepper Shakers or the Phoenix
or anything besides The Whip and the Italian Trapeze.

A few trips from now,
I'll go to Knoebels for the last time
because each time is filled with the dread
of more and more friends and family

wanting to go on the rollercoasters
that I'm too scared to ride,
and soon the groups we went with
will stop coordinating trips
and we'll quietly stop going altogether.

No Faith

A replica of the image of
Our Lady of Guadalupe
(you'd know it if you saw it)
was touring the Catholic church circuit
sometime when I was in 8th grade,
and I was tasked with
helping the tour coordinators
get the heavy wooden boards
that the image was mounted on
into St. Canicus
and set up in front of the altar.

The coordinators thanked us,
and invited us to touch the replica,
which is something people won't get to do
during the actual presentation later that day.

They told us,
three 13-year-old boys
who make up sins for confession
and only go to mass
because our parents make us,
that those with strong faith
can feel Mary's heartbeat
when they press two fingers to her ribs.

My friends go first,
and nod after a pause
when asked if they felt it.

I touch the tips
of my pointer and middle fingers
to the same spot they did,
and I wait for something to happen,

and I'm still here
15 years later
waiting for something that might not ever happen,
everyone's experiences
blurring by in time-lapse around me,
wondering if certain real things
that I thought
were supposed to be a part of life
are actually guaranteed to happen,
or if the bus that's 15 minutes late
is broken down
and already taken to the junkyard
to be sold as scraps,
which will be explained to me
years later with a condescending
"oh, nobody told you?"

I'm thumbing through
all of the permutations
of strata of peer pressure
that caused our responses,
whether they actually felt it and I was the only liar
or if they lied because they thought I'd feel it,
or if we're all lying because
the coordinators made it seem
like we'd be less of a Catholic
if we didn't feel something,
and I'm wondering if anyone
ever actually felt anything at all,
or if it's just liars all the way down,
being poseurs for God.

Gettysburg

The 2nd most tragic thing
to happen in Gettysburg, PA
was that I had to walk around the Civil War battlefields
with an ingrown toenail
on the big toe of my right foot
during my 8th grade field trip,
and then had to sit next to a teacher
on the bus ride back to the school,
which meant I couldn't listen to my CD player
because I didn't want Mr. Dowd
to overhear my *ELO Greatest Hits* CD,
and I couldn't play my GameBoy Color
because I didn't want Mr. Dowd
to ask me about *Pokémon Silver*,
so I sat there in silence instead
and wiggled my toe up and down
so I could get a temporary relief from pain
as the 150-year-old ghosts
phased through our charter bus
as we headed to General Pickett's Buffet for lunch.

The Beach

My favorite thing
about stores and restaurants
at the beach
that you've vacationed to
for the past 20 years
with your family

is that they're all old
and sort of crummy
and that the carpets in those places
clearly haven't been replaced recently,

and you look forward to
going to the same ones each time,
because the places
never appear to age at all
and it seems like
it's only been days
since you were first there,
and not years.

They serve as a safe zone
where you escape time,
and can lose sense of
how old you are
as easily as you lose sense of
which way you're facing in the shower
when you're shampooing your hair
and have your eyes glued shut
as you turn and turn and turn
to keep all sides of your body
equally warm under the hot shower water.

The shops all have
the same shelves and displays

overflowing
with the same souvenirs,
like straw beach mats
and starfish and sand dollars
and little message-in-a-bottle bottles,

and the screen-printing t-shirt shops have
pastel t-shirts with the beach name,
and off-white t-shirts
with beach-going cats and dogs on the front
and their butts on the back,
and other t-shirts that your Uncle Harry
would wear while grilling back home
that have something cheesy like
"10 Rules When I Drink Beer"
or a cartoon of what 1998
thought a hot girl looked like
and some joke about
how you can't tolerate your wife anymore.

The boardwalk walks you take
wearing a light hoodie and shorts
on your way back from dinner
when the waves still seem
impossibly calming yet loud
and the breeze hugs your ears
are the time machine of walks.

Tolerating Time

You need to dance with time
as it careens around a large ballroom
in the way a steam locomotive
derails and skids
and has its cars crinkle up at the couplings
in every single dream you've ever had
involving steam locomotives.

You need to match the chaos
in the way speeding cars next to you
on the highway
make it seem like
you're not going that fast at all.

Lionel

The freight trains flew by
at the train station in Fredericksburg
and I could feel myself
inching
closer
to the edge
of the platform
to peek down at the rails
breathing in
and out
as the wheels passed over,

and I remembered my brief stint
as a conductor of the Lionel trains
on the train sets my Pappap got for me
(but really for him)
over a couple consecutive Christmases
and how I'd push them too fast
around the corners
and they'd derail off the platform,
tumbling onto the floor
and startling our cats,

and I hoped that the conductor
of this real train
wasn't the type of person
to play NASCAR video games
and turn around at the start of the race
and do the laps backwards
like I was.

To-Do

I've pinpointed the moment
when you start doing things
because they're simply things that people do:

it was when
Superman underwear briefs
and Rugrats Band-Aids
turned into
tighty whities
and plain beige bandages,

because I don't have to be tricked
into doing what I have to do
and there's no need to incentivize
something that's necessary forever,

and I'm left seeking something more substantial
that's not done by all
in order to get the public praise,

and anything expected is mindlessly done
with no frills at all,
part of a compulsory checklist
on the eternal clipboard.

Glimpse

Dust fills the negative space
where a jar of pennies used to sit,
just like I try to recall
what was once well-thought out
and vivid in my mind,
but now all I can see of it
is shadows
and the reflection
in the corner of my eye
in a stainless steel appliance.

As soon as the moment happens,
I know it's waiting to get lost and buried
by the more recent moments,
and it's only a matter of time
until it's gone forever
if I don't save it or act upon it,
with a ticking timer hidden behind it,
the way the tickets to *WWE Raw* will be gone
from my Ticketmaster cart
if I don't check out
in the next 5 minutes and 30 seconds.

Brain-RW

I'm ushered into my house
by the polite chill air
similar to the air
that gives you the feeling
of when you first enter
your beach hotel room
and you plop the bags on the bed
and decide to,
for some reason,
go on a quest to find the ice machine.

There are so many
stressors pressing in
outside of this brief relief
so it's as reassuring
as a pat on the back
after you miss an easy spike
in a volleyball game
and your team just wants you
to keep trying your best
until you rotate positions enough
that you're standing on the sideline
flipping the scoreboard flaps.

Once you return
from your cartographical adventure
of looking out hallway windows at the parking lot
and finding the good vending machine,
you sit at the edge of your bed
and realize how much work
is ahead of your temporary pause
and store it safely in your mind
next to the instances
where you realized
you weren't good at doing ollies

on your skateboard
and that the girl you like
doesn't notice all of the effort
that you put forth
into accidentally walking
out of school at the same time as her,
so you hide it all away
until you're laying in bed
one Saturday morning
weeks later
and unearth these memories
and cast away the responsibilities
that go with hanging onto the past,
because it's hard to stretch on a Twister mat
and you can't always reach what you want
from where you're sitting,
so you take these memories
and use them as fuel
for motivation to get up
and get ready
and do something
that will write over
the negativity that you let fester.

Antiques Roadshow

You are a mid-19th century
Navajo Ute First Phase blanket

and I am the quirky college-professor-looking appraiser
from PBS' *Antiques Roadshow*
struggling to get through the segment
because I know what you're worth
(and you've just been draped over the back of a chair,
an unassuming decoration in someone else's life),
and I'm searching for the words
to break the news
that I understand the monumentality of the
significance and existence and presence
of you.

BILLY

I want
your favorite books
and my favorite books
to mingle
on a BILLY bookshelf from IKEA
that we assembled
together.

Spring

She's the first day of spring weather
when you have the urge to go outside
to play catch and organize a kickball game.

Vulnerable

we're all video game bosses,

going through
repeated
predictable
patterns
of actions
to defeat a tiny little foe
with a bottomless bag of swords and stunts
and infinite lives and infinite restarts
that seems to keeps coming at us,

opening our chest to expose our hearts
and turning our backs to show the crack
in our armor that we know is there
that we offer to others
in a show of our fragility,
like a hermit crab between shells,
like how MMA fighters
tap gloves at the start of a round
when they're going to be
punching each other's faces
in a few seconds,
hoping we can have
a little truce.

i can be me when i'm alone
at a red light
with the *Revolver* CD
at a too-high volume,
and i want to
be me with you, too,
and i want you to be
suffocatingly you,

so we can bask in each other,
no filter,
like your first exhale
on a cold winter night
when you realize
the world is silent
and waiting for you.

Her Hug

was looser this time.

Across

Only when you sit
on opposite sides of a table
can you most easily
look the other person
directly in the eyes.

Vacant

Every time I realize
that I don't have something,
it hurts as if I lost it,
even if I never really had it
to begin with.

Maybe

I hate "maybe"

because "maybe"
is just a "no"

that has yet to emerge
from its chrysalis
of letting-you-down-softly.

Traded In

I am
a bottom shelf
stuffed animal prize
in a carnival game
that's too easy to win.

CD-R

No matter how well
you sequence songs
on a mix CD,
she'll never like you back.

Good Night

My full bed
feels pretty empty.

En Garde

You don't need to carry a sword,
but at least wear some armor.

Should've

The best opportunities
to do all the things you wanted
have happened
at unfathomably impossible times.

Your soulmate
died in Gaul
in 200 B.C.

She Is My Factory Settings

I dutifully unfold
a paperclip
and reach behind my head
to press the little red button
in a tiny recessed space
at the nape of my neck
then wait to reboot
to erase
the memories
of her and
of how I've been reset before,
which are both
hopefully for the best.

Let's try this again,
because this version of me
doesn't yet know
that the end result
is still preordained
and that I'll be back here again
within 12-15 months.

Strongly Agree

I feel like,
when I reflect,
I'm taking one of those
online satisfaction surveys
that you get in your email
with a promise
that you'll be entered into a raffle
to win a $50 gift card,
but you never really find out
who wins the gift card
because maybe there wasn't
a gift card
at all.

I'm always wondering where I am
on the spectrum of

> not having something to look forward to
> and
> not having something to dread,

and I'm wondering what shade of neutrality
I'd rather experience.

Sequel

There is a nearly-indescribable feeling
of unlimited potential
teeming in every waiting second
of every new moment
when you experience a sequel
that is different from the first
and better than the first
while still being close enough to the first.

I'm sitting in the grass
next to the marshmallow-looking
wrapped bales of hay
that make up a little maze
at the farm we're visiting
on a field trip in 5th grade,
and I have a ham sandwich in my lap,
resting on my blue ABVM sweatpants
and I'm booting up *Pokémon Silver*,
and it feels like a bottle of Coca-Cola
fizzing to life
as the experience unfurls,
and I know how great it will be
because I already paged through
Prima's Official Strategy Guide
and had the new color palettes
of the towns and Pokémon
sooth my eyes.

The new familiarity
coaxes us all along,
and it's comforting to have
when there are so many new unknowns
that are cold dead ends
that make you awkwardly turn around
using someone's driveway

and grumble under your breath
about how that wasn't the right way,
and you reassure yourself
that you will definitely
stay on the main road next time
and not take a turn
that looked like a shortcut on Google Maps
when you glanced at it quickly
at a stop light 5 minutes ago.

Loudon County

Driving back from Virginia to Pennsylvania,
I pulled over to the side of the road,
shook hands with the sunrise,
and then we went our separate ways.

Staples

Fake reason I went to Staples:
buy printer ink

Real reason I went to Staples:
to drive swiftly
through a chill fall night's air
with windows down and music loud

Trees

The leaves of a tree only fall
when they have
singularly
individually
solely
specifically
been looked at.

The fall foliage
is when they've become desperate
after a summer of people
sitting under them and looking away
and only looking up to find a lost cat or kite
and the leaves need a shortcut to attention.

People will appreciate the shade
but not each leaf that makes it possible.

The leaves will burn bright
and crack out of existence
when they scream for attention
and get it
and die.

Some people live their lives like these leaves,
but I don't know if it's any better being a conifer,
risking being cut down
and decorated
and thrown out on the curb in January.

Quest

The rain is slowing down
as he leans into his first step
entering the crosswalk
with his elbows locked
and arms straight,
hands plunged into
the kangaroo pockets
of an old Penn State hoodie,
his chin tucked down to sternum,
shoulders shrugged up
to protect his neck
on his jaunt to Rite Aid
to get some ibuprofen
before they close.

Snow Above

it's always snowing in heaven,
the heavy falling flakes
illuminated by a street light,
the clumps of crystals
sticking to the road
without a fuss,
sparkling despite
the slightly-filled-in
car tire tracks
that left an imprint
a couple minutes ago.

The Goal of Everything in Life Is Experiencing Warmth

I'm drowning
in blankets and hoodies,
and I'm wearing slippers
that aren't mine.

I'm currently in a chrysalis
of comfiness and toastiness.

Parallel Lines

I hope my life
is never in shambles enough
that I have to pass someone on
a double yellow,

because I've always seen that the car that passes me,
no matter how fast he drove,
ends up at the red light
only 1 car ahead of me.

Aggressive Drivers

One of these days
I want to sit down with
one of those people
that drive on highways
by furiously serpentining
between all of the lanes
without a care or turn signal in the world
as if their car is a hot piece of pasta
that was dredged from the boiling pot
and they're batting it back and forth
between their hands
to cool it down a bit
before tasting it
to see if it's firm
or al dente.

I would ask them why they don't
just ride a rollercoaster
or do meth
or something else that gives them
a rush or a high
that doesn't involve making me fear for my life
when I picture a violent accident
from a dash cam that was posted online,
but happening in real life in front of me,
and I hope I would also react
as gracefully as those drivers do,
curtly cursing in Russian
and driving on around the crash,
slightly perturbed
by this mild inconvenience in my commute.

Roadside Memorials

How long do they wait
before taking down
the roadside memorials
for those that died there
in an accident I didn't read about
that warranted
crosses affixed to the tree
and stuffed animals
strewn on the ground
and dirt bike company logos
flown on flags from the branches
and names spray painted on boards
and sun-faded photos
of the deceased
under a page protector
framed with popsicle sticks?

Cemetery

New churches are both
pessimistic and optimistic
when they buy huge tracts of land
for their cemeteries.

On one hand,
their first parishioner's death
is sad and mournful,
but it also legitimizes the parish
like when a struggling actor
gets his first IMDb credit.

Lost Kids

I can't imagine
being one of those
National Center
for Missing & Exploited Children
lost kids
whose faces are on
the pair of Chiclet gum machines
that stood at the exit
to Marone's Café
in Girardville
where my mom
always got the shrimp scampi

and I got the chicken fingers,
and I had to face the lost kids
on our way out
and remind them
that I just had my favorite meal
from my favorite restaurant
and they might not even be alive.

In Memoriam

The montage at award ceremonies
of the people who died this year
isn't fair,

because we can't show
the people born this year
that will
make a mark in the future.

Stack Overflow

I don’t care
about what happens to me
after I die;
I want to know
what happened to me
before I was born.

Doors

I fuss about details
and I hate the logistics
of things like spices in food
and anything that has to be done with precision
such as screws and plugs and connections
because I don't have enough attention
to think with that much concentration
and with that much sustained focus,

and my brain decides
that this is great fuel for dreams
and has a recurring element be
that doors never shut correctly
because they're 2 inches too short width-wise
and the latch doesn't reach the lockplate,
and the hinges are slightly loose,
so the door sways a bit up and down
and there's simply no teamwork at all
between all of the parts of a door
that make a door do its door things.

Double-Layered Options

I don't like being asked,
in familiar situations
about familiar topics,
previously unasked questions,
because it makes me aware
of how I took for granted
that that question was always previously answered
or assumed for me.

When I was babysat by my Aunt Barb and Uncle Harry,
they made me spaghetti
and asked if I wanted it cut.

I said yes,
because I assumed
that my parents always cut it for me
because I never got
1 single long spaghetto
when I ate it with sauce with them
or with 5 gallons of butter and sprinkle cheese
when I ate it with my mammam.

I got my spaghetti,
which had cut up hot dogs in it
(but that was expected)
and the strands of spaghetti
were 1 to 2 inches long
and nearly impossible to
do that trademark spaghetti forktwirl to.

More recently,
I went to Zoës Kitchen
and got the potato salad as a side
as I had done at least 3 times prior,
and this time they asked how I wanted it,

and I didn't know there were any options,
but the type I always got was the default
and the type I got from then on
was the better "grilled" style.

You don't know if you don't ask
and you don't know you don't know to ask
until someone asks you first
in order to awaken you
to the options hidden from you
behind a cover
like a fuse box in the basement.

Corner of My Eye

There's a single piece of glitter
somehow stuck to the side
of the bridge of my nose,
and I can only see it
when I'm turned at a certain angle
and looking a certain way,

but I don't want to get up
and go look in a mirror,
because I don't want to see
that I also have to shave
and that I've been picking at
my left eyebrow too much
and that it's starting
to be on the verge of
looking sparse in the middle,

so I've been running my left pointer finger
over where it appears to be,
but I'm coming up empty
and decide to stop trying
because I'll forget it's even there
until I see it again in 5 minutes
and hope this time I'll nab it
without somehow flicking it
like a tiddlywink squidger disc
and having it land in a slam dunk
right on my pupil.

Lame Duck Weekend

I'm staring at the
abstract art piece
created with the
fork rake patterns
through the remnants
of the sauce
from the penne pasta
from last night's dinner
that I reheated
as leftovers
and ate this morning
before I showered,

and I'm existing
in the purgatory of
the weekend
on a Sunday
just before noon,
where the weekend
is still alive,
but the last 12 hours
are almost written off
as a complete loss

because the specter
of Monday
is waiting nicely
behind me,
in the same way
you wait in line
at the grocery store
while the person
in front of you
types in her
credit card PIN

and the cashier
says his goodbyes
and reminds her
how much money
she saved by
using her bonus card,
followed by his
script of greetings
where you notice
that he said
they were "good"
to the last customer,
but somehow
only "fine" for you,

and you rethink
your own
script of responses
for when you
go to the
grocery store next,
and how you should
stop seeming so
chipper to the cashier
by saying you're
"great."

Citizen Shopper

I form a kinship
with the people at the grocery store
that apparently got there
about the same time I did,
and also like to serpentine
up and down each aisle,
even if there's nothing
on their list there,
because maybe the breadcrumbs
or the parmesan cheese
are in an aisle
that you wouldn't think they were in,
and you don't really want to
have to retrace your steps
in the frantic search
where you park your cart next to
some display for cocktail sauce
because you need nothing holding you back
from the strong-gaited march
back to the "cooking solutions" aisle
for the 3rd time this trip
to see if they actually have yeast
in the little packets,
or if that's a thing that's hidden somewhere
high up on a shelf
in the greeting card aisle,
or somewhere else illogical like that.

I'm stuffing the 5-foot-long
ribbon of a receipt
into my wallet
and I look over
at the checkout next to me
and make eye contact
with the guy in a dress shirt

who I caught searching
for Velveeta mac and cheese
while I grabbed a 4-pack of tuna
from the shelf next to him
20 minutes ago
in aisle 5.

100 Deeds for Everyone in the World

Pick up the saltine cracker wrapper
when no one is looking.

Flash your high beams
at the car that's been debating moving over
for the past half-mile.

Fetch the volleyball
that your team dug errantly to the right
and roll it to the other side
so they can serve it again.

Stay after the event
and ask "where does this go?"
instead of "do you need help?"

Grab a cart
from the cart return.

Start the day off
with a net positive favor
so that humanity has a deed to spare
in a take-a-penny-leave-a-penny kind of way
where they're unknowingly further away
from playing from behind
when someone else
decides to be a jerk unprovokedly.

Do these deeds regardless
of what others are doing
because someone has to be the first one
to stop clapping at a play
and start to stand up at the movies
as a semi-unnoticed cue
that other people need to change states.

I Hate Golfers

(and I could probably just end that there)

who over-complicate the game further
with their penalties for grounding clubs in sand
and rules for how/where you should drop your ball
and fuss over hitting
"provisional balls"
because your tee shot
hooked several miles deep into evergreen trees
and you're probably not going to find it,
and the course management is snooty enough
to not allow you to play by winter rules
where you can just kick your ball off of tree roots
or drop your ball
where your best-case-scenario estimate is
for where your ball ended up
and everyone is like "ok."

There are many things
that are inherently relaxing
because of their components,
and they are often ruined
in a too-many-cooks
type of ordeal.

Simply put,
golfing is a really fun thing to do
with your friends
after 2 p.m. on a Saturday
when you rent the pull carts
and do the 9-hole course,
because it's $7 a person,
and you can't have 2 hours of fun
anywhere else for that cheap.

You can change some of the factors
with a delicate touch
and the same finesse it takes
to dial a shower knob
and find "warm,"
but you're typing on a keyboard
with a hammer
when you add
more restrictions and rules.

What I'm saying is this:
you look stupid
with your matching pastel blue
Titleist polo and fitted hat,
and I'm not impressed
by your bag full of fancy Nike drivers
and $5 balls with cores made of Unununium
or something just as gimmicky.

Thoughts Kept in a Shadow Box

These poems are just
conversations that I hope I'll have later,
or ones that I wish I'd had before.

Mitosis

I need some of my poems
to undergo mitosis
and become 2 separate beings
because I'm trying to say too much at once,
and I know how brevity is the soul of wit
and all that crap,
and I always tell other people the proverb of
"if you chase two rabbits, both will get away,"
which a surprisingly high number of people
don't understand,
which might explain a lot about their
suffocatingly high-energy work ethic,

so I'm torn

between

making sure nothing goes unsaid,
because that then causes another mood of poetry
where I try to say the things I wish I'd said before,
in the "spirit of the stairs" sort of way,
so I need to slowly bleed out the steam
via tweets across a couple days
or poems that won't escape my drafts folder
as if writing out the most precise version of my thoughts
will unlock some new gamemode in life
where I get to do
the idealistic version
of what I think would have happened
if I did say what I wanted before
as if I'm entering cheat codes
into *NFL Blitz*
to turn off interceptions
or turn on big head mode

and

cutting myself off at the right time,
which is something I am horrendously horrendous at,
which is why the guy working the bar
at the wedding at the former bank
recommended I drink some water
instead of getting another Yuengling and cranberry vodka,
which is what I'd been ordering all night
because I saw people with dates getting 2 drinks
and thought that I could do the same
without any suspicion,
outside of the fact that I was dancing the polka
to a song that was probably an Irish song
and not a Polish polka song
considering the bride and groom were both Irish
and not at all Polish,
and I'm feeling like something can't be short and quick
because then it's not substantial enough
and I need to throw more words at an idea
to beef it up some more,
while also hoping I'm not
diluting the original spirit of the idea
too much.

Drafts

It's hard to give up on a poem
and leave it in my "drafts" folder
while the rest of my poems are finished
and sequenced into the final lineup for the book,
but, then again,
you can't cook a meal
with every ingredient in your pantry,
so I'm saving them as projects for later.

Some poems are a car on a jack in my garage
whose parts are already delivered
and it's a matter of time
until I can get it fixed and running again.

Others are cars sitting in the tall grass
next to a fenced-in garage
on an alley
that faces the railroad tracks,
and they will probably sit there,
despite all my best intentions,
while I work on something actually worthwhile.

Some of them are only the wheels,
the rest of the car
to be scavenged and assembled later
when I find a junkyard well-stocked enough to do so.

One of my poems
is a single screw-of-a-moment
that I didn't even know
was a piece of a car at all.

I'll consider this poem a tribute that gives me closure
for all of those unrealized compositions
that are probably going to sit in that folder forever

as they gather dust
and negative memories
of how I tried to tweak the tone
and add some spark with different lines
and go from a narrative to a
"just-give-the-gist-of-the-feelings" format
where you're reading the Spark Notes
of an e.e. cummings poem
that was based on an impressionist painting
of how some guy described the scene
and you're several degrees removed from what was there
and only left with the essence
as if you saw it out of the corner of your eye
while driving past at a fast speed,
yet nothing made it better.

Three Poems About Meatlovers Pizza

One time
I ordered a meatlovers pizza,
but only got a meatlikers pizza.

If I ordered
a meatlovers pizza
and the guy at the pizza place said,
"what, do you love meat or something?"
I would never order it again.

I would like the Supreme Court more
if they were called
the Meatlovers Court.

Product Placement

One of my recurring nightmares
is that I can only hold cheeseburgers
the way people in commercials for cheeseburgers
hold cheeseburgers.

The burger is perfect,
and I'm not allowed to bite it
to let the burger realize its potential
because that would break its perfection.

Pills

It's quite difficult for me
to accept some truths that
might be a "hard pill to swallow"

because I have a really bad gag reflex
and can never bring myself
to actually swallow a pill
to send it on its way
like the Log Flume at Knoebels,

so whenever I go to the doctor
on my own like a big boy
to have a grown-up problem diagnosed,
I have to ask for the amoxicillin
as a pink bubblegum-flavored suspension,

and I get the same feeling
as when I order the chicken fingers
from the kids' menu at a restaurant,
which I have also done
with the same amount of lack of shame.

That amoxicillin is delicious,
and so are those chicken fingers.

Advent Calendar

I want to buy an Advent calendar,
but each door opens up
to a full tube
of cheddar cheese Pringles.

Blackmail

Good blackmail on anyone
would be a video
of when they bite into a
fresh-out-of-the-microwave Hot Pocket
and a slice of too-hot ham
slips out
and touches their lip,
causing them to whimper
and spasm out of their chair
like a 10-year-old boy
unsuccessfully
trying to ollie on his skateboard
in his driveway
for the 42nd time today.

Wawa

The things that I am familiar with
are the absolute peak of perfection,
and your local stores and methods
are complete garbage
and how dare you even mention them to me,
the person who is the arbiter of
which local gas station chain
makes the best made-to-order hoagies
no matter how late at night you go there.

Volcano

The pyroclastic flow of puke
slid softly down my chin.

Vocations

It's so hard getting a job these days,
especially compared to how easy it was
in the 17th century

where you could be a doctor
and be completely wrong about everything
and not wash your hands at all
and think that draining someone's blood
is a way to drain away their sickness

or where you could be a cartographer
and draw lines anywhere you wanted
and say that California was an island
and that giant chubby disembodied heads exhaling
are what caused winds in the open oceans.

But I Don't Want to Be Called a Dick

I want to be a private eye
so I can sit in a dark room
behind a big desk
and talk to dames
on my rotary phone
while patiently waiting
for a parcel to arrive from New York
that is wrapped in paper and twine
that contains stolen jewelry
from the scene of the murder of
the mayor's ex-wife.

Hmmm

I wonder if cats know they're cats.

Māo

This is a poem
that I'm writing at a party
when I'm trying
to convince
my roommate's sister
to buy me some acid
in exchange
for babysitting her cat.

Sort of Like a Cat Café

I want to go to a bar
that has cats you can pet
while you do shots of vodka
served in souvenir shot glasses
from places you've never been.

Kitty Cat Delinquent

I know it sounds funny,
but I just can't find my cat.
I think she ran away tonight.
All of her other cat friends are feral
and don't contribute to society.
They will not vote in the upcoming election,
but mostly 'cause they don't have ID.
That's kind of whack that ID is required,
but I guess it's for the greater good.
I don't wanna own a kitty cat delinquent.
What will all my neighbors then think of me?
Raising my cats without any loving?
You cannot be any further from the truth.
I love my cats more than I love my own parents,
and I don't see anything wrong with that.
You're a hypocrite if you choose to judge me.
Let he who is without sin throw the first stone.

I lost my kitty.
Been missing since Sunday morning.
I lost my kitty
and I'm just crying and mourning.

But really, guys, I'm serious,
she might not be okay out there.
She had her claws taken out
and she can't defend herself.
I know there's some strays around our block,
and God knows what they'll do
if they see a new cat around.
And her fur will probably get really dirty,
especially if she goes exploring around in bushes
and gets caked with mud and leaves and stuff.
I don't wanna have to shave her back again.
That already happened once

when she was in the backyard
and ran through the hose
and tried to scratch her back on the mulch
and it just got really messy.
That wasn't good for anyone involved.

I lost my kitty.
Been missing since Sunday morning.
I lost my kitty
and I'm just crying and mourning.

Psss pss pss pss
Where are you, kitty?
Pss pss pss.
Kitty!
Ah!
I found you!
There you are!
Let me pet your chin, come here.
Come here!
I'm so happy you're safe!
Where were you?
You are a dirty kitty.
That's okay, take a tubby.
Go eat,
I'll get you more wet food.

I found my kitty.
I found her early this morning.
I found my kitty
and now I can stop mourning.

Lost Cats

I can't stand
when I see all of the missing cats
posted on the
"lost animal"
Facebook pages
and think of how many cats
are simultaneously gone from their homes,
roaming gutters,
skirting along hedges,
peeking at the sky
waiting for dawn to break,

but then I'm sort of at ease with it,
because I think about the hobo cats,
the permanently stray cats,
who may have once been owned,
but long forgot their person-given name
after too many seasons outside,

and I think about those hobo cats
giving aid and quarter to the lost ones
with no front claws
who are startled at the approaching garbage truck
and scamper away when a car scoots by.

It can no longer be a coincidence
that all of these cats are out missing,
because I saw 10 new postings yesterday,
and 15 more tonight,
and I'm sure 20 more tomorrow,
because I think these cats are playing hooky on purpose
to get a taste of adventure
and go camping under a deck for just one night
because they know how many chin scritchins
and banquets of wet food

will await them
as they feign nervousness
trotting back to their front door,
perfectly timed in the morning
when their owners are going to work
and are resigned to the fact
that their loved cat is truly missing
and gone out and about,
and that maybe he/she is even dead,
but now they're back,
and they wanna knock stuff
off the kitchen island with impunity,
because no one will ever
take their existence for granted again.

The Most Important Penny in the World

The cashier at Turkey Hill
failed the friendship test
when my total was $4.01
and I left with 99¢ of change
in my pocket.

Conversely,
when a total ended in .99,
I was going to tell the McDonald's drive-thru cashier
to keep the penny change,
but then I saw
that she was going to keep the penny,
and that made me want the penny,
so I did a stutter step on the brakes
like I'm heel-toeing a bass drum pedal
as we both realized
what the other expected us to do.

Semi-Numismatic

I like old coins.

Not the "whoa, a 1902 silver dollar
from the Philadelphia mint" old coins,
but the "penny from 1954 in your change"
kind of old coins.

I Don't Know What to Wear

Men in the 1940s
wore their suit pants
up to their clavicles
and their ties dragged on the ground,
so what I'm saying
is that acceptable fashion trends
change over time
and you can't stop me
from wearing this wrestling t-shirt
to your cousin's wedding.

Rikishi

Like a sumo wrestler
tossing salt to purify the *dohyō* (ring),
I toss my crumpled socks
onto my freshly cleaned-off bedroom floor.

Hi-Rise

My time spent in apartment complex basements
provided a lot of fuel for nightmares
of labyrinthine pipe-filled explorations.

Impromptu Drive-In

I completely understand
moths' almost suicidal
devotion to being as close as possible
to any source of light

because I've been very close
to getting into car accidents
while passing a van
filled with a family of 4
and trying to see
what movie they're playing
on a fold-down TV screen
for their kids in the back seat.

Saturn

Some days
you drive around
using your turn signals,
coming to complete stops at stop signs,
waving on other people at intersections,
being a model citizen of the road,

and some days
you're the jerk
in the slightly-rusted-if-you-look-really-close
4-cylinder sedan
flooring it
at the bottom of a hill
to pass someone.

Mr. Herman

My ultimate job
is whatever Pee-wee Herman did
to be able to afford his playhouse
and have time to visit there
and engage in playhouse-related shenanigans.

Junk Drawer

I believe
that a house should have
a large bookshelf
stocked with books
just as much as it should have
a junk drawer in the kitchen
overflowing with
Chinese and pizza place menus
to the point that they jam the drawer
and form a canopy over
the purple magnetic BINGO chip wand,
loose bread ties,
and stray AAAs
that slide and shift
every time you
shut the drawer with your hip.

Commandment Number 9

When Moses came down
from Mount Sinai,
he held in his hands
the 2 records
of The Beatles' *White Album.*

Queen

If you play
"We Will Rock You"
and it's not followed by
"We Are the Champions,"
then you're committing a mortal sin
and you need to confess that.

Cussing

The nicest thing
someone can do
in a social situation
is to curse first

because it lets you remove
parts of the façade
that you had up
where you pretended like
you also didn't curse,
and you can move one step closer
to being who you actually are.

Ciggy Butt Brains

I'm gonna print out
a bunch of "cool award" certificates
to hand out to the kids
I see smoking at 7 a.m.
on their walk to school.

Feet

One time in college
I joked with a girl
that I liked feet,

so she jokingly
had me massage hers,

and eventually
it wasn't a joke at all anymore.

Movies from 5 Years Ago on TV at 11 p.m.

The best part
of watching movies on TV
that come on after the show
you just got done watching

is the tension and suspense
when you see the opening

"X presents,
in association with Y,
a Z film"

for 2 minutes
as you resist the urge
to press "guide" on the remote
before the movie title
finally shows up.

Count Down

There are
12 months in a year,
11 something or others,
10 dimes in a dollar,
9 squares in tic-tac-toe,
8 slices in pizza,
7 days in a week,
6 beers in a pack,
5, uh, points on a star,
4 quarters in a dollar,
3 sections of a folded letter,
2 pieces of my broken heart, and
1 poem concept
that I thought would be much better
than it actually ended up being.

Aesthetic-less

I hate those poems
With each new line
Starting with
A capitalized letter,
Even though there
Is no reason to do so,
And even when words
That normally
Wouldn't get capitalized
In titles are now
Getting capitalized
At the start of a
New line.

The poet just
Got lazy with the
"Automatically
Capitalize the
First letter of
Each line"
Feature in Word
And didn't care
Enough to give you
A poem
With capitalization
That makes sense.

Typing this poem brought me
Physical pain.
Sorry.

No One Cares About Trivial Things Some People Get Their Doctorates In

I bet some nerd out there
has written a formula
with all sorts of Greek letters
to find the surface area
of a fortune cookie.

Primordial Sounds

I don't know the first sound
to ever happen in the world,

but I hope it was something equally as pleasing
as the sounds of
walking on gravel rocks
the size of marbles,
or a water bottle
being filled
and howling
as the water gets closer to the top,
or keys being fumbled with
on the other side of the front door
when you're expecting your parents
to be coming home
with the Chinese food they got for you,
or a golf ball
kerplunking into the hole
right after the girl you took
mini-golfing
laughs her trademark laugh.

(The world will end
with the sound
of hundreds of ironing boards
creaking open,
that much I'm sure.)

Prospecting

I wish anything earlier in my life
prepared me for adulthood
as much as digging through containers
for the LEGO piece I needed
prepared me for
digging through unsorted laundry baskets
for a matching dress sock.

I Guess This Is Growing Up

"Santa isn't real"
wasn't as childhood-ruining of a revelation
as "most limousines in NYC
aren't filled with famous people,
it's just normal people inside."

Secrets

The only thing better
than telling a secret
is telling people
that you have one.

"Big Time" Brandon Rush

The *Back to the Future* trilogy
had the time traveling message
that you shouldn't know
about your future self
because that will cause you
to act differently in the present
in an attempt to create the seen future,
while inadvertently disrupting that future
because you now made different choices
than you originally would have
if you didn't have an ultimate goal to work towards.

You can't approach Ebenezer Scrooge
in the lobby before the play
and tell him that he'll buy a turkey for Tiny Tim
on Christmas morning
because that's cruel
and messes with time
as it's supposed to play out.

My friend "Big Time" Brandon Rush
is a new professional wrestler
getting ready for his debut tonight
in a battle royal
where the winner of the match
is the last guy remaining in the ring,
and that will be whoever
sold the most tickets to the show.

He lets out an "ehhh, it's close"
when we ask if he has a good shot of winning
as we chat during intermission.

We sit back down and get ready for him
to still have a strong showing,

not knowing that he's going to
win the whole thing
by suplexing the second-to-last guy
and then tossing him over the top rope.

He already won the match when he was talking to us,
but we just didn't experience it yet
because he hadn't done the intermediate steps required
to realize the predetermined future.

He was the Tralfamadorians from *Slaughterhouse Five*,
or, to pick an example from a book that doesn't suck,
Dr. Manahttan from *Watchmen*
(but without the being blue and naked
with his wiener hanging out part).

A $5 Organ from Blum's

I realized that I had too much stuff
when I was trying to lift
into my dad's truck bed
a 200lb organ
that I won at Blum's Bid Board auction house
for $5

and we were pushing 30 minutes
of moving
and carrying
and lifting
and tilting
until we gave up on being gentle
and somehow heaved it up
with the emergency muscle-tearing strength
that would normally be reserved
for getting a boulder off a loved one
during a hike in the Grand Canyon.

The organ didn't even work,
and we had to pay to drop it off at the dump,
so I spent a lot of money on nothing
just because I liked
having things and winning things,
but it was worth it because
I had to have a critical moment like this
that would make me finally realize
that I had an unhealthy relationship with stuff.

It was also worth it
because the organ came with a sweet organ bench
that I'm currently using in my bathroom
as a little table under whose seat lid
I can keep washcloths,

but I think that initial epiphany alone
would have given me my money's worth, too.

DeSales Homecoming '17

For all 4 years of college,
I did enough vetting of parties
where I always had
a quorum of close friends
that I could stand near
and bounce between
when meandering among
the basement, kitchen, and living room
of the rowhome
originally inhabited by
immigrant workers
of Bethlehem Steel.

It was a big blow to my ego
when I found myself
at homecoming this year
sitting in an empty parking space
with 3 über-acquaintances
and only 2 close friends
(Murph and his wife Ann),
and the conversation was going bad
more quickly than
an opened bag of pre-chopped salad.

There are new dorms
and academic buildings
and multi-purpose athletic fields
and intersections to get to
all the new creations
that have been built over the past 6 years,
but I continued on undaunted
because the recurring dream-motif
where I'm in a familiar place
but there are extra staircases and doors
that lead to extra levels of attics and basements

had properly prepared me
for being somewhere familiar,
but having it be some
Twilight Zone version of the place.

The girl I made out with 6 Halloweens ago
(and then made grilled cheeses for)
was ignoring me
after we made eye contact
across 3 rows of cars
because she was gallivanting around
with her fiancé,
who was the guy she started dating
1 month after we hooked up,
even though she told me she wasn't ready
for a boyfriend again,
because she only broke up
with her last one
a couple weeks before that.

We left to get beer to make this more fun,
and the über-acquaintances suggested
that we get pizza too,
so we went on a nostalgic journey,
going back to Se-Wy-Co,
the beer distributor
where we got 3 kegs in 2011
for the failed homecoming party,
and stopping to pick up pizza
at Mario's, the place next door,
where I'd stop to get slices
on Wednesday afternoons
when my classes were done by noon.

Everyone in the parking space
pitched in for the pizza,
so Murph and I made our money back,

which is in stark contrast to
how we fared
after the 3-keg homecoming party in 2011.

Some girls joined our group,
and they looked like extras
in a movie set at a college homecoming,
and I couldn't imagine that
they had identities
and fears
and wants,
because I was just so overwhelmed
by these unfamiliar people
in this very familiar place,
and it was too much of a shock to take in,
so I just waited for it to pass.

One of the über-acquaintances
shotgunned a beer,
spraying it on us all,
prompting us to
chug our beers,
grab a slice of pizza,
and abandon the rest of the pie
so that we could flee to the soccer field
to watch the guys' game.

My college's claim to fame
is that Steve from *Blue's Clues*
went there
(but never graduated),
but besides that,
no one even knows that it exists at all.

There are small colleges
all around the country just like mine,
with unique concentrated stories,

dorm names,
and urban legends of their own,
like the specks of dust
that Horton finds,
each housing its own world,
and they all keep doing their thing
and aren't in any way frozen in time
waiting for you to come back
and resume some paused memories,
and this whole experience was a good reminder
that you shouldn't look back at memories,
but instead to the side in quick glances
the same way you check for cars
before changing lanes on the highway.

Home

Junior year of high school
was a turning point
where some kids got their licenses
and started driving home from school
while others still sat
on the sparsely-populated bus.

The cars were held back
in the parking lot
until the buses left,
and you'd see the parade of cars
passing the buses
at the first stretch of road
without double yellow lines.

They'd act nonchalant,
zooming by us,
staring dead ahead,
just so they could be
one vehicle ahead of us
when they got stuck at
the first red light in town, too.

One day, a senior passed us
in his 4-cylinder sedan,
flooring it at the bottom of a hill,
and the bus driver asked us,
but no one in particular,
where he was in a hurry to,
and we said "home,"
and he crafted
a proverb
that was a surprisingly dense nugget of wisdom
compared to where it came from.

He said:

Home is where you go
when you've got
no place left to go.

ABOUT THE AUTHOR

Tyler moved to Virginia 3 years ago and is trying his best to water his garden of acquaintances well enough that some friends will sprout.

He asked a coworker out on a date this year and she said yes, but he didn't use the word "date" when he asked, and then when they finally found a day that worked with her, she asked who else was going to go and he realized that she didn't think he was actually asking her out on a date.

One time Tyler made a joke during a teacher league kickball game when he got to third base about how he never got to third base before and the thirdbaseman thought he wasn't intentionally making a double entendre and it upset him.

He somehow still doesn't have a cat.

Follow Tyler on Twitter and Instagram:
@puttertutters

Follow Puttertutters Press on Instagram:
@puttertutterspress

MORE FROM PUTTERTUTTERS PRESS

available from Amazon, Barnes & Noble,
or asking Tyler directly if he can sell you a copy because he does still have a couple extras that he can sell to you and he can even sign it if you want, it's up to you

Reminiscing Over That One Time That We Both Forgot

A collection of 26 poems about relaxing when you can, rebuffing others when you need to, and reminiscing all of the time.

$9

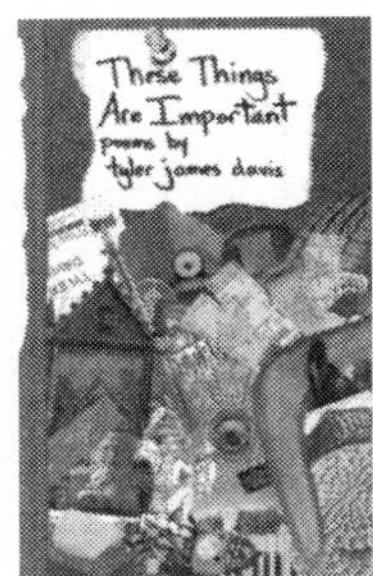

These Things Are Important

52 new poems about all the things Tyler misses from when he was younger and how he has an unhealthy attachment to physical objects that are portkeys to memories he wishes he could return to.

$11

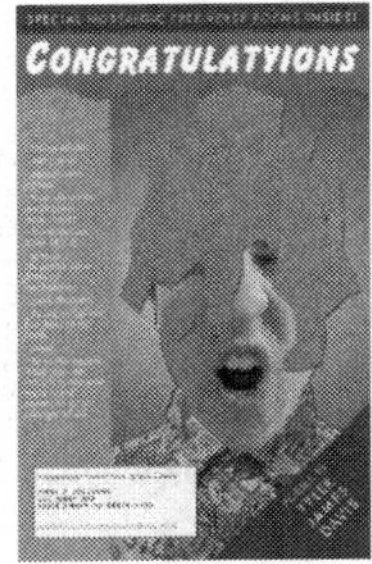

Congratulatyions

This is the book you are currently holding in your hands right now.

$12

Made in the USA
Columbia, SC
11 August 2018